ADVENTURES IN THE ABYSS

A DYSTOPIAN ACTIVITY BOOK FOR THE MODERN AGE

Dozens of puzzles, games, coloring pages, and quips to entertain you in the hellscape.

Written by
Meredith Erin

Illustrated by
Matt Snow

Copyright © 2022 by Meredith Erin and Matt Snow
All rights reserved. No portion of this book may be reproduced in any form without written permission from the publisher.

ISBN: 978-1-7365435-1-1
Library of Congress Cataloging-in-Publication Data
is available for this title.

Originally published in softcover by Boredwalk in 2022

Written by Meredith Erin and Matt Snow
Editing by Matt Snow
Proofreading by Matt Snow
Cover design, layout, and illustrations
by Matt Snow for Boredwalk
Printed in Canada

Boredwalk
9120 Norwalk Blvd
Santa Fe Springs CA 90670
www.boredwalk.com

IF YOU DON'T LAUGH, YOU'LL CRY

We spend so much of our time lamenting the dystopian conditions of the modern age, but truth be told, human existence has been plagued by darkness as far back as we go. It's almost like we're an inherently troubled species. Will it get better? Probably not, but at least we can laugh about it!

We designed this book to help you find a few laughs in the endlessly bleak reality we all share. Some of these activities are perfect for entertaining yourself, and some are fun to share with a friend. Whether you're using this book to pass the time in an underground bunker after the robot uprising decimates existence on the surface or simply giving your strained rods and cones a break from the glare of your phone screen, we hope these activities will keep you entertained.

While we can't tell you that it will change, we can tell you you're not alone in the hell world. So grab your favorite colored and No. 2 pencils and get ready to puzzle, color, and create your way through these activities we've designed for the most discerning denizens of the dystopia!

-Meredith & Matt

WORD SEARCH: SORROWFUL SAGA

Find the will to live (and a few other things) in the puzzle below!

~~Will to live~~	~~Pessimism~~	~~Hopeless~~	~~Anxiety~~
~~Hellscape~~	~~Serotonin~~	~~Distress~~	~~Rejection~~
~~Trauma~~	~~Self-loathing~~	~~Suffering~~	~~Isolation~~
~~Dystopia~~	~~Disappointment~~	~~Bleak~~	~~Panic~~
~~Ennui~~	~~Dysfunction~~	~~Crisis~~	~~Dopamine~~
~~Depression~~	~~Misery~~	~~Doom~~	~~Crying~~

HOPELESS HAIKU: ROBOT UPRISING EDITION

Add some beauty to this little corner of the abyss with poetry! On this page, write a haiku about a robot uprising.

Tip: Haiku is a Japanese poetic form comprised of three lines. The first line has five syllables, the second line has seven syllables, and the last line has five syllables.

_____

_____

_____

MATH PUZZLE: GRAVITY

Once humanity has ruined this planet we'll be off to ruin another one. Will our new home be an improvement? Not likely! We'll end up on some remaindered planet no other life forms wanted, a fate we'll richly deserve. Solve the puzzle below to determine how much the average adult will weigh on the new planet with sub-optimal gravitational pull.

🪐(10) × 🪐(10) = 100

40 ÷ 🪐(10) = 👽(4)

👽(4) ÷ 🛸(2) = 🛸(2)

100 − (40 × 🛸(2)) = ✴(20)

✴(20) + 🛸(2) = ☄(22)

100 + ☄(22) = ? 122

FUTURE NEWS: SPACE WAR

Fill in the blanks below with the requested word or phrase. Then plug those words into the corresponding blanks on the next page to complete the news article from the future! *(Note: This activity is best done with a friend/captive.)*

Number: _____

Adjective: _____

Giant Corporation: _____

Verb: _____

Celebrity: _____

Adjective: _____

Noun: _____

Celebrity: _____

Noun (plural): _____

Noun (plural): _____

Noun (plural): _____

Celebrity: _____

Number: _____

EARTH PRESIDENT KIM KARDASHIAN XVII TO SEND MILLIONS MORE TROOPS TO SPACE AMID GROWING TENSIONS IN THE MILKY WAY GALAXY

President Kardashian XVII has ordered _____ million Earth-based troops to space, demonstrating Earth's _____ commitment to intergalactic peace.

GlaxoSmithKline and _____, the respective occupants of the Delta and Gamma quadrants of the galaxy, objected to the move, complaining it infringed on their right to _____ off-world.

GlaxoSmithKline spokesperson, _____, called the deployment "_____" and vowed there would be "_____."

Kardashian XVII had a tense exchange with GlaxoSmithKline CEO _____ on Tuesday. The newly-installed CEO demanded Kardashian XVII draw down troops and allow the competing corporate _____ to settle the dispute on their own terms. Both parties have advocated for a battle of _____ to resolve their territorial dispute.

The Kardashian XVII administration maintains that diplomatic solutions are still possible if the feuding parties will put _____ aside.

Planet House Secretary _____ told reporters today that President Kardashian XVII has spent _____ weeks drafting proposals for a cease fire.

TOXIC TECHNOLOGY CROSSWORD: CLUES

Modern technological advances were *supposed* to deliver a charmed existence full of conveniences, comfort, and plentiful resources for all. Instead of living like The Jetsons, we're really living like characters in a hell dimension. Let's solve a puzzle that's all about the worst aspects of life in the 21st century!

DOWN:

1. Threatening senior citizens with arrest unless they buy gift cards

2. Online dictionary you'll need as you age to figure out WTF the kids are talking about

3. "Don't forget to like & subscribe"

5. Facebook's virtual reality

6. This is why your identity got stolen

8. How dating is done in the modern age

11. "This one simple trick doctors don't want you to know!"

12. Why I never answer my phone anymore

14. Dopamine hit everyone seeks online

15. Not-so-delicious online trackers

16. Professing concern for causes online while actually exhibiting no real effort or commitment in practice

19. The intentional spread of fake news

22. Jeff Bezos, Elon Musk, Bill Gates, Warren Buffett, and Jack Ma

25. The great pretender's favorite online pastime

ACROSS:

4. The kind of hyper-productivity expected of us in the modern age

7. Nasty commenters on the internet

9. No hospital system, electrical grid, or consumer data is safe from them

10. The worst section of any online article

11. Blockchain-based currencies

13. Selfie sticks and detox teas

17. Press 9 if you know your party's extension, press 1 for sales, press 2 for support, press 3 for a directory

18. Porn, but for spite

20. In 2010 the US Supreme Court affirmed the First Amendment rights of these non-humans

21. A spammer's target

23. A weekly report that will show you how much of your life you're wasting staring at your phone

24. Introduced your baby boomer aunt to conspiracy theories

26. Digital junk mail

TOXIC TECHNOLOGY CROSSWORD: PUZZLE

SPOT THE DIFFERENCE

The illustrations below and on the next page may *look* the same, but they actually contain slight differences. See if you can spot all ten of the objects that are either missing or different from those in the illustration on the next page!

SPOT THE DIFFERENCE (CONT'D)

WORD JUMBLE: DYSTOPIAN AUTHORS

Unscramble the names of the famous dystopian fiction writers below:

1. oeggre owlrle

2. aermratg dowtao

3. ary yaubrbrd

4. gh ewlsl

5. nytohan ssbgreu

6. hilipp k ckdi

7. seetnr ilecn

8. esnuazn soinlcl

9. lsauod luxehy

10. rilnicas silwe

11. ruauls k el iung

12. nhoj myadhwn

13. znrfa aafkk

14. iddav sortef calwlae

15. urkt tugvenon

16. aiwmlli idgongl

HELL WORLD HOMOGRAPHS

Homographs are words with the same spelling, but different meaning (and sometimes different pronunciation). For example, a spread for toast AND interminable urban traffic would be a…jam. All the clues below have homographic answers:

1. The amount of hope there is for our climate AND how long it takes for a mega corp to bring in more cash than the average person makes all year:

_____

2. Influencers' stock and trade AND an elusive emotional state:

_____

3. The future of our planet if we keep chopping down all the trees AND what billionaires plan to do about it:

_____

4. A conspiracy theorist's reaction to generally accepted science AND coupons:

_____

5. Swiping left on a dating profile AND trash:

_____

HELL WORLD HOMOGRAPHS (CONT'D)

6. A topic of study in school AND a citizen under an authoritarian ruler:

_____

7. A weapon AND an exclusive group you'll never be a member of:

_____

8. Something to burn in a tyrannical society AND a way to make a restaurant reservation:

_____

9. A place for environmental spills to wash up AND financial institutions who got bailed out by the US government during The Great Recession:

_____

10. You can kiss the ruler's one of these AND use it to cause civil rights and privacy concerns:

_____

PHONE TREE TRAP

Need assistance from an actual human? Good luck! You're going to need it to navigate the corporate phone tree below. Don't forget to listen to the full recording, because you just KNOW those menu options have changed!

HOPELESS HAIKU: DEADLY DINOS EDITION

Add some beauty to this little corner of the abyss with poetry! On this page, write a haiku about the chaos that ensues when scientists reanimate the dinosaurs.

Tip: Haiku is a Japanese poetic form comprised of three lines. The first line has five syllables, the second line has seven syllables, and the last line has five syllables.

_____

_____

_____

CRYPTOGRAMS: DE-MOTIVATIONAL QUOTE EDITION

Decode the message! Each letter in the phrase has been replaced with a random number. Try to decode the message using the clues that have already been revealed!

A	B	C	D	E	F	G	H	I	J	K	L	M	N	O	P	Q	R	S	T	U	V	W	X	Y	Z
				17				4						18											

_ E _ _ _ I _ _ _ I _ E _ _ O
23 17 2 8 11 4 9   12 4 6 17   22 18

_ O E I _ _ _ _ _ _ _ _ I _ _
18 22 17   4 2   15 11 5 7 13 4 22 10

BLEAKEST BINGO

How many of these hellish scenarios do you have experience with? See if you can score bingo by checking off each tile below that applies to you!

Lost a full day in line at the DMV, IRS, or similar government agency.	Paid an exorbitant sum for medical services, even with insurance.	Had your identity stolen.	Been catfished online.	Charged an overdraft fee. (Yay! Paying more money for not having enough money!)
Been victimized with no consequences for the perpetrator.	Lost a loved one to a cult.	Unjustly profiled by law enforcement, transit authority, etc.	Diagnosed with an illness caused by environmental factors (e.g., pollution, lead in water, etc.)	Spent time trying to prove to a robot that you're not a robot (e.g., Captchas)
Waited in line for several hours to vote.	Been hacked (e.g., your computer was hacked, your email account was hacked, etc.)	Been cyberstalked, cyberbullied, doxxed, or swatted.	Participated in an attack drill at school (e.g., mass shooting, nuclear strike, etc.)	Spent time correcting an error in your credit report.
Your student loan balance is/was double the figure you originally borrowed.	Worked while on vacation.	Were forced to pay a large fee to cancel a service or membership you no longer wanted.	Googled your symptoms and convinced yourself you were dying.	Been subjected to a baseless search by the state.
Couldn't get a job without experience, but couldn't gain experience without getting a job.	Didn't have enough credit to get a loan or card, but couldn't build credit without a loan or card.	Stopped answering your phone because robots won't stop calling it.	Took a drug to solve one problem that caused a new problem, for which you needed more drugs.	Arrested or attacked by agents of the state for peacefully protesting.

WHO SAID IT?

Draw a line from each quote below to the author who wrote it!

1. "There will come a time when it isn't 'They're spying on me through my phone' anymore. Eventually, it will be 'My phone is spying on me.'"

    Kurt Vonnegut

2. "If you gaze long enough into an abyss, the abyss will gaze back into you."

    Margaret Atwood

3. "That was when they suspended the Constitution. They said it would be temporary. There wasn't even any rioting in the streets. People stayed home at night, watching television, looking for some direction. There wasn't even an enemy you could put your finger on."

    L.M. Montgomery

4. "So, in the end, above ground you must have the Haves, pursuing pleasure and comfort and beauty, and below ground the Have-nots, the Workers getting continually adapted to the conditions of their labour."

    Aldous Huxley

    Philip K. Dick

5. "If you want a picture of the future, imagine a boot stamping on a human face — forever."

    T.S. Eliot

6. "This is the way the world ends. Not with a bang but a whimper."

    Charles Dickens

7. "The mass of men lead lives of quiet desperation. What is called resignation is confirmed desperation."

    H.G. Wells

8. "My life is a perfect graveyard of buried hopes."

9. "It was the season of light, it was the season of darkness, it was the spring of hope, it was the winter of despair."

    George Orwell

10. "America is the wealthiest nation on Earth, but its people are mainly poor, and poor Americans are urged to hate themselves."

    Friedrich Nietzsche

11. "Maybe this world is another planet's hell."

    Henry David Thoreau

CRYPTOGRAMS: CORNER OFFICE IN HELL EDITION

Decode the message! Each letter in the phrase has been replaced with a random number. Try to decode the message using the clues that have already been revealed!

A	B	C	D	E	F	G	H	I	J	K	L	M	N	O	P	Q	R	S	T	U	V	W	X	Y	Z
4				1								25													

```
 A  _  _  _  _  E  _        M  E  E  _  _  _  _
 4 18 21 17  5  1 24       25  1  1 17 15 18 16

 _  A  _  _        _  _  _  _  _        _  A  _  E
17  5  4 17       23 21 26 19 22        5  4  7  1

          _  E  E  _        A  _
          9  1  1 18        4 18

       _  E  _  E  _        _  _  A  _
      15 18  1 20 20  1    23 17 26  4 19

       _  _  _  E  A  M        _  _  _  _
       6 23 24  1  4 25       15 18 17 21

             _  E  _        _  _  _  _
            17  5  1        7 21 15 22
```

21

MATH PUZZLE: TRILLIONAIRES

Solve the puzzle to reveal the number of metric tons of carbon billionaires will pollute the planet with as they race to become Earth's first trillionaires.

$$\text{barrel} + \text{barrel} = \text{pump}$$

$$\text{barrel} \times \text{pump} = 50$$

$$50 \times \text{pump} = \text{boat}$$

$$\text{boat} \times \text{pump} = \text{rocket}$$

$$\text{rocket} + \text{boat} + \text{pump} = \,?$$

HELLSCAPE HISTORY CROSSWORD: CLUES

Sure, the modern age is terrible, but let's be honest: humanity has been terrible throughout its history. Whether we're harpooning whales or burning each other at the stake, our species has *been* the worst. Let's take a trip down bad memory lane with this puzzle inspired by dystopian living in the days of yore!

DOWN:

1. Tens of millions died during his blood-thirsty reign as Mongolian Emperor

2. The most fatal (and metal!) pandemic in recorded human history

3. It's good to be the king (of England, when you can have two of your six wives executed, I guess)

4. Armed combatants providing entertainment in Ancient Rome

5. 1990 Concrete Blonde album title referencing a dubious historical medical practice

6. Late 20th century Chilean dictator

10. Credited with "modernizing" China (and causing over 40 million deaths)

12. Illegal CIA human experimentation program launched in the 1950s

17. PTSD, World War I-style

18. Stocks (and not the investor variety)

20. Rumor has it he "fiddled" while Rome burned

ACROSS:

7. She was arrested for voting in the 1872 presidential election

8. Suspected of heresy, this stargazing polymath from Pisa died under house arrest

9. More than 18% of the industrial labor force in the US by 1900

11. Mid-20th century moral panic of a purple variety

13. The subject of George Takei's graphic memoir *They Called Us Enemy*

14. US President with blood (and a Trail of Tears) on his hands

15. How people often lost their heads in 18th century France (and beyond)

16. Someone shoulda been fired for this bombing strategy during the Vietnam War

17. Legal in the US until the passage of the Thirteenth Amendment

19. The site of 1989 student-led demonstrations that ended in a government-sponsored massacre

21. Peasants under feudalism

22. Burned at the stake for heresy in 1431; canonized as a saint in 1920

HELLSCAPE HISTORY CROSSWORD: PUZZLE

24

LOGIC PUZZLE: HORRIBLE HISTORY REBORN

Scientists have decided to clone the worst possible people! These dystopian figures are going to be duplicated one at a time, so solve this puzzle to determine the order in which these villains will be cloned. In case you're not familiar with these notorious historical monsters, you'll find a short dossier here about each of them:

Attila the Hun
• Leader of an empire centered in present-day Hungary from 434-453 AD.
• One of the most feared enemies of Western and Eastern Roman Empires.
• By the time he died, he was known as the "scourge of god," and his death was cheered in what was left of the Roman Empire.

Genghis Khan
• First emperor of the Mongol Empire, with a reign lasting from 1206-1227.
• Launched the Mongol invasions, ultimately conquered most of Eurasia, and caused the deaths of millions.

Vlad the Impaler
• 15th century Romanian ruler also known as Vlad Dracula.
• Infamous for his penchant for torture, mutilation, and mass murder.
• Fond of impaling his victims, he partly inspired the titular character in Bram Stoker's 1897 novel *Dracula*.

Elizabeth Báthory
• Late 16th/early 17th century Hungarian noblewoman and purported serial killer.
• Legends claim she bathed in the blood of virgins to retain her youth.

Vladimir Lenin
• Communist head of the Soviet Russian government from 1917-1924.
• Suppressed opposition in a violent campaign during which tens of thousands were killed or interned in concentration camps.

Joseph Stalin
• Served as General Secretary of the Communist Party of the Soviet Union from 1922-1952.
• During his totalitarian regime he oversaw mass repression, ethnic cleansing, and hundreds of thousands of executions.
• Millions were imprisoned in labor camps and died in famines during his reign.

Mao Zedong
• During his reign in China from 1943-1976, this communist ruler imprisoned millions in labor camps.
• He created the largest genocide in history, causing the deaths of 40-70 million people through forced labor, executions, and starvation.

LOGIC PUZZLE: HORRIBLE HISTORY REBORN

- A vampire film could be based on either the first or seventh clone
- The second and sixth clones both imprisoned millions in labor camps
- The third and seventh clone were Eastern European rulers
- The fourth and sixth clones were Russian
- The second and fifth clones were Asian
- The second, fourth, and sixth clones were originally active in the 20th century

	Attila the Hun	Genghis Khan	Vlad the Impaler	Elizabeth Báthory	Vladimir Lenin	Joseph Stalin	Mao Zedong
FIRST							
SECOND							
THIRD							
FOURTH							
FIFTH							
SIXTH							
SEVENTH							

MISSPELLING MISERY

Another imperfection in our deeply flawed world? Why not! Circle the misspelled word or phrase on each line below!

1. abyss | apocalypse | authoretarian

2. catastraphe | censorship | colonialism

3. depression | dispair | dictator

4. feudalism | feifdom | fascism

5. hopeless | hegemony | hysetria

6. imperialism | internment | inquisiition

7. melancholly | miserable | martial law

8. nightmares | nihilism | nuclaer waste

9. pessimism | propaganda | pollution

10. sorrow | stigma | sufferring

11. tyranny | truama | totalitarian

12. ventrue capitalist | weary | Xanax

TWO TRUTHS AND ONE LIE (PART 1)

In each puzzle below you'll find two true headlines and one that's made up. Identify the fake one!

PUZZLE 1

a.) Michigan judge berates 72 year old with cancer for failing to maintain his lawn

b.) Wisconsin mayor blackmailed for nudes by rogue bot

c.) Indian couple plans virtual wedding in the Metaverse

PUZZLE 2

a.) Amazon files patent that would use facial recognition technology to create database of "suspicious" people

b.) Former judge sent thousands of kids to jail while accepting millions in kickbacks from for-profit prisons

c.) Pentagon explores building a detention center on Mars

PUZZLE 3

a.) IRS will require facial recognition scans to access tax returns

b.) Tribunal concludes China forcefully harvests organs from detainees

c.) Alabama school district has children arrested for overdue school lunch debt

PUZZLE 4

a.) Blind man fails citizenship test after being refused a version of the test in Braille

b.) Brain implant will allow employers to monitor employee health and productivity

c.) Immigration and Customs Enforcement Director claims ICE cannot be compared to Nazis since they're "just following orders"

DEAR ALIEN OVERLORDS...

Aliens have landed and they're considering vaporizing Earth. Our planet has been nothing but trouble, and they don't trust humanity not to destroy the galaxy in pursuit of our ever-growing off-world ambitions.

Fill in the blanks below with the requested word or phrase. Then plug those words into the corresponding blanks on the next page to edit a letter to the aliens intended to convince them we're a species worth saving. We're not, of course, but it's worth a shot! *(Note: This activity is best done with a friend/captive.)*

Adjective: _____

Adjective: _____

Adjective: _____

Adjective: _____

Something Found on Earth: _____

Something Found on Earth: _____

Noun: _____

Noun: _____

Adjective: _____

Noun: _____

Adjective: _____

Noun: _____

Period of Time: _____

Adjective: _____

Period of Time: _____

Verb: _____

Adjective: _____

TO WHOM IT MAY CONCERN:

Greetings, Visitors!

We trust that your _____ journey to our humble planet has been _____ and _____. While you tour Earth you'll notice some of its _____ features. For example, the _____, _____, and the remaining wildlife we have not yet driven to extinction.

While I can understand your desire to destroy our species, if you give us another chance we'd love to try to get our act together. In the last year alone we've accomplished these impressive feats:

• We've found a new 100% renewable energy source derived from _____

• We've moved from engaging in violent warfare amongst ourselves to instead settling our disputes through _____

• We've stamped out a number of _____ diseases with vaccines and the use of _____

We know we have a long way to go before becoming ideal citizens of the universe, but we're making an/a _____ effort and hope you'll take this into account as you consider our fate. We admire your advanced civilization and your impressive _____. We believe we could learn so much from you.

We can also agree to stay out of space for _____, while we work on becoming a _____ species.

We hope you'll consider giving us a grace period of _____ to satisfy your demands. I am confident we can _____ into the future with a renewed commitment to becoming productive members of galactic society. I know you are busy and _____, so thank you for taking the time to read this plea.

Sincerely,
The People of Earth

WORD SEARCH: MISOGYNY

You won't have to look far to find the misogyny in this puzzle!

```
E Q C I S M K A H M B J Z A A T R C X Z
C D W O T W U N S H Y S T E R I A L X N
U M F P N M B V Y S K N I X V C Y Y H W
S X Y T O Y R H N D A M A N S P L A I N
C R P G R R K D K S L U T S H A M I N G
H O D R O O F I E S W L L V H E G O E R
X A B O R W Z S J I H I M T J Y X Z M M
C V R J U W M M J H H V A B C B Z I F D
M A X A E C D I S C R I M I N A T I O N
H N L G S C H L T D C J B P E U N M A Y
L O C M H S T E M O M M Y T R A C K I M
A S U V D K M I E R E V E N G E P O R N
D M Q S Z O F E F Z Q S I R U N R R I S
Y I U W E Y W G N I P A T R I A R C H Y
L S P A S W W N E T C N J U Q P U Z V F
I O S G E X O A I W K A M A L E G A Z E
K G K E X V I R G I N I T Y T E S T E N
E Y I G I M R D K L A K A I N H E K Y O
D N R A S T E A L T H I N G O B D F C Y
Y Y T P M C A T C A L L I N G N I O P D
```

Objectification	Discrimination	Slut Shaming	Catcalling
Harassment	Stealthing	Patriarchy	Mansplain
Virginity Test	Mommytrack	Male Gaze	Calm Down
Housework	Misogyny	Roofies	Assault
Hysteria	Douche	Revenge Porn	Ladylike
Upskirt	Wage Gap	Sexism	Smile

WAYS TO KILL TIME

Whether we're trapped on a rocket to Mars after destroying Earth or biding our time in a fallout shelter after the next World War, we'll need a way to entertain ourselves without the usual creature comforts we enjoy like Netflix, cocktail bars, and music festivals.

Brainstorm a list of analog ways you're going to stay entertained once the terrible choices of humanity destroy the way of life to which we've grown accustomed:

WORD JUMBLE: AUTHORITARIAN SOCIETY

Unscramble the words in the authoritarian society themed puzzle below:

1. ejitiuscn
2. oscespnrih
3. dttorica
4. idnamoiiintt
5. fiamssc
6. anpgraaodp
7. rablo pacm
8. rlamtia awl
9. sspooeprni
10. ericntupeos
11. iaaotttalinr
12. nyntary
13. rvleaueilsnc
14. iihoiprtnbo
15. yuectlr
16. ionneerclat

CRYPTOGRAMS: ALREADY TIRED TOMORROW EDITION

Decode the message! Each letter in the phrase has been replaced with a random number. Try to decode the message using the clues that have already been revealed!

A	B	C	D	E	F	G	H	I	J	K	L	M	N	O	P	Q	R	S	T	U	V	W	X	Y	Z
17				22										5											

E V E R Y T H I N G   B E I N G
22 20 22 21 10 14 12 19 23 2   7 22 19 23 2

T H E   A B S O L U T E
14 12 22   17 7 18 5 8 9 14 22

W O R S T   A T   A L L
4 5 21 18 14   17 14   17 8 8

T I M E S   I S
14 19 13 22 18   19 18

E X H A U S T I N G
22 3 12 17 9 18 14 19 23 2

HOPELESS HAIKU: BRAIN IMPLANT EDITION

Add some beauty to this little corner of the abyss with poetry! On this page, write a haiku about a new social network that you can implant directly into your brain.

Tip: Haiku is a Japanese poetic form comprised of three lines. The first line has five syllables, the second line has seven syllables, and the last line has five syllables.

_____

_____

_____

LET'S HOST A DYSTOPIAN MOVIE NIGHT!

You've been hired to host a dystopian triple-feature! Make a list of the movies you'd like to present and write a short summary of each for your soon-to-be viewers!

Example:
Gattaca
Thanks to Jerome Vincent's parents' insistence on being quaint, he was born without genetic engineering, and is now trapped in an inferior physical form. Refusing to have his hopes of space travel dashed, Vincent assumes the identity of a paralyzed Olympic athlete, all in an attempt to con his way into the elite class and finally get on a damn space rocket.

Movie #1: _____

Summary: _____
_____
_____
_____
_____

Movie #2: _____

Summary: _____
_____
_____
_____
_____

Movie #3: _____

Summary: _____
_____
_____
_____
_____

RULES FOR BABY ALIEN CARE

How will our petty human concerns finally be superseded? Perhaps while humans battle for world domination an alien race will beat us to the punch and become our new overlords.

In this alternate reality imagine our new societal obligation is baby alien duty. Our space-faring masters would be much too busy taking over the universe to be bothered with the mundanity of caring for their young, so you're going to have to do it.

Using the prompts below and on the next page, create instructions for taking care of these infant aliens.

Alien Race Name
("Hey shrieking slimy tentacled thing" is a mouthful — and pretty rude — so give these diminutive extraterrestrials a suitable name.)

Feeding Instructions
(What do little aliens eat? Plant material? Human blood? Aluminum siding? Fill it in below, along with how to prepare their meals and how often to feed them.)

Exercise
(A growing alien needs plenty of exercise to grow up strong and continue their species' intergalactic reign of terror. What type of exercise do the tykes prefer? Bench pressing 18 wheelers? Swimming with polar bears? Describe their preferred exercise regimen and any equipment needed for the activity.)

RULES FOR BABY ALIEN CARE (CONT'D)

Rest
(How often does the little one need to sleep and what are its preferred sleeping conditions? Do they sleep upside-down hanging from the rafters like bats? Or perhaps in a metal tube that emits transmissions from their home planet? Fill it in below.)

Entertainment
(What do little aliens do for fun? Whether it's reading Chaucer novels or destroying you in a heated chess match, describe how to best keep junior amused below.)

Habits & Words of Caution
(What else should anyone caring for a baby alien know? Do they devour furniture or tear open wormholes to another plane of existence when bored? Jot down the details below.)

SCRAMBLED RHYMES

Unscramble these dystopian phrases that rhyme!

Example: an aquatic mammal after pollution blots out the sun would be a leap elawh (pale whale)

Scrambled Clues	**Unscrambled Answers**
1. Future tyrant: **letra rodttirac**	1. _____
2. A depressed friend: **mgul mhuc**	2. _____
3. An idle mob: **rdbeo eorhd**	3. _____
4. Bad news story after bad news story: **akelb kaster**	4. _____
5. Education, in a punitive atmosphere: **lucre losoch**	5. _____

SCRAMBLED RHYMES (CONT'D)

Scrambled Clues

Unscrambled Answers

6. A social media troll limited to 280 characters:

    wrettit trtecri

6. _____

7. A drug to blot out reality and try to relax:

    lichl lipl

7. _____

8. Sadness 24 hours later:

    rrootmwo roowrs

8. _____

9. Unsolicited dick pics in your direct messages:

    duer dune

9. _____

10. Burning the garbage will lead to these unwanted remnants:

    shart has

10. _____

WORD SEARCH: CORPORATE DYSTOPIA

Find the dystopian elements of the corporate world in the puzzle below!

```
W C O N F E R E N C E C A L L I P Q L T X S Q M U
P S R Y Y T P E A T K R P X L Y N I B Y H X V E Z
I Y C E Z D V Q Y G O L D E N H A N D C U F F S H
N P F C Q N S V I E V N D K U E D C P Y C P M H J
G C M I L O R S N C O F N F F L C B N U G B R G
M W I R S T X V Y T P Q P J S D O P Y Z M P I L X
E S C C P I A A K Z R C E O Y T L V I X S T N E I
O F R L G F K C I N O P R T N G L L F U U T B A X
P F O E T I W T Y X D F F K E Y A E K O M P O R K
H I M B L C T I R V U S O X R T B V V Y A D X N F
B H A A M A C O K R C T R Y G K O E N Z V N G I D
E Q N C A T C N L D T A M Q I T R R H S Q M T N J
S P A K O I U I M O I T A Q Z H A A J A R S O G L
T D G M G O T T I W V U N H E O T G V X H B U S Z
P U E G F N N E N N I S C S W U I E J S X A C W S
R E S L A S G M G S T R E S N G O Z J L Q N H K L
A K D H I L J S A I Y E R Q K H N F N D E D B X E
C M Z A D V Q M Y Z U P E S B T A G I L E W A C G
T Q V J S M E B B E F O V V J L C M S L Z I S J R
I J T C G A P R S L R R I J X E V N E I R D E B E
C W Z A C O P N A W L T E D Y A V K R T C T F V Q
E Q D C P U K K N B U Q W N X D J N Y F R H B I U
Y L X R L L A T U Y L G T W B E C B Y K K I U I W
C N C M W R D V V U W E B T P R I X J A B A C K J
I P H S T W B N U T V G H C X Z N O Q P W A L S G
```

Performance Review
Notifications
Best Practice
Circle Back
Downsize
ASAP

Conference Call
Productivity
Deliverable
Synergize
Leverage
Bandwidth

Collaboration
Golden Handcuffs
Status Report
Touch Base
Agile
Ping Me

Thought Leader
Action Items
Micromanage
Learnings
Metrics
Inbox

DESIGN YOUR METAVERSE AVATAR!

If the technocrats have their way, we'll abandon our physical lives for a virtual reality. Who else is excited to become a sedentary orb of a creature permanently hooked into cyberspace? Imagine your avatar in the new virtual world and use the prompts below to describe it.

Appearance
(What does virtual you look like? Glowing orange eyes? Tall as a telephone pole? Always dressed in head-to-toe leather? Describe your virtual look below!)

Hangouts
(Where does your avatar spend their time? Can they be found flying above the mountains like a bird or exploring the depths of the ocean? Your flesh prison might not be going anywhere, but your avatar will be going virtually everywhere they please!)

Associates
(What kind of crowd will your avatar hang out with? Cyberpunks? Outdoor adventurers? Space farers? Describe your avatar's social life below!)

Special Abilities
(Flight? Superhuman speed? Pyrokinesis? What will your avatar be able to do that your puny human form is incapable of?)

FUTURE NEWS: MOIST GARBAGE

Fill in the blanks below with the requested word or phrase. Then plug those words into the corresponding blanks on the next page to complete the news article from the future! *(Note: This activity is best done with a friend/captive.)*

Number: _____

Adjective: _____

Adjective: _____

Noun: _____

State: _____

Celebrity: _____

Adjective: _____

Adjective: _____

Adjective: _____

Number (1-100): _____

Noun: _____

Celebrity: _____

Adjective: _____

Number: _____

Adjective: _____

Adjective: _____

43

GREAT PACIFIC GARBAGE PATCH FILES FOR STATEHOOD

Residents of the Great Pacific Garbage Patch have voted to be recognized as a state and have demanded admission to the United States. For _____ centuries the isolated but growing, and now-sentient, Patch has become a _____ hub for members of the _____ Brotherhood, a faith-based group who've been making pilgrimages to the Patch since it began issuing predictions about the _____.

American voters are split on the issue, _____ Governor _____ told the New England Times "The _____ people of my state don't want to see _____ people taking advantage of our _____ system."

_____% of voters in a NewsMega poll said the United States has larger problems like the _____ crisis and that this isn't the time to be considering admitting another sentient garbage patch to the country.

President _____ has expressed support for the Patch's statehood ambition and urged voters to keep a(n) _____ mind with regard to this initiative.

In order to qualify for statehood the Patch will have to gain the support of at least _____ states. Pollsters predict the effort is likely to fail due to lack of support from _____ women, who make up a significant number of voters in _____ states.

FIND THE MISSING LETTERS

Prove you've got a top notch dystopian lexicon by solving the puzzle below!

Example: depre_ _ion
aby_ _
darkne_ _
Answer: ss

1. gr_ _f
   d_ _d
   harr_ _d

1. Missing Letters:
   _____

2. bl_ _k
   d_ _th
   nucl_ _r

2. Missing Letters:
   _____

3. su_ _en
   bu_ _y
   po_ _ute

3. Missing Letters:
   _____

4. ca_ _e
   disa_ _er
   _ _ate

4. Missing Letters:
   _____

5. cr_ _is
   pr_ _on
   m_ _ery

5. Missing Letters:
   _____

45

FIND THE MISSING LETTERS (CONT'D)

6. cens_ _
   h_ _ror
   terr_ _

6. Missing Letters:

_____

7. _ _ying
   _ _uel
   auto_ _at

7. Missing Letters:

_____

8. cur_ _w
   _ _udal
   suf_ _r

8. Missing Letters:

_____

9. _ _ber
   _ _nical
   priva_ _

9. Missing Letters:

_____

10. gu_ _g
    _ _bor
    s_ _ve

10. Missing Letters:

_____

SHELTER SEARCH

Well, we finally did it — we blew it up! Time to find shelter in the post-apocalyptic wasteland. Hurry, though! Radiation has already turned some of your neighbors into flesh-eating mutants, and they're feeling peckish.

YOU ARE THE LAW!

From tyrannical dictatorships to bumbling democracies, governments often play a role in making our reality more dystopian. If we think things are bad today, just imagine what fresh hell they might come up with in the future! Fill in your ideas below:

A New Draconian Punishment
(Public humiliation? Sentenced to death by shark battle? What new methods will governments employ to punish law breakers?)

A New Way to Select a President or Prime Minister
(Random selection like jury duty? Only the wealthy get a vote? What terrible system will they think of next to install new heads of state?)

A New Prohibition
(What's getting banned? Cursing in public? Wearing white after Labor Day? Jot it down below so you can brag that you called it first!)

YOU ARE THE LAW! (CONT'D)

A New Mandate
(What is the government requiring everyone to do? Sign up for trash heap shoveling? Wear heavy weights like the characters in Kurt Vonnegut's "Harrison Bergeron?" Just think of the new levels of horrible we could reach!)

A New Tax Law
(Taxes are meant to fund things that serve the public interest, but they're not always implemented in a way that is just. Perhaps they'll come up with a new tax on life saving medication or eliminate all taxes for the ultra wealthy? What new tax law will they invent to worsen our society?)

An End to an Existing Prohibition
(Fewer restrictions can be a good thing, but not always. Maybe they'll allow unelected corporate executives to sit in the legislature and vote on new laws, or eliminate more environmental protections. What prohibitions that serve the public interest might they strike down in the future?)

DYSTOPIAN FICTION CROSSWORD: CLUES

They say art imitates life, and the art of dystopian fiction is no different. If you've read the classics or seen hit apocalyptic thrillers out of Hollywood, you'll ace this crossword puzzle with clues related to some of the most famous dystopian fiction in cinematic and literary history!

DOWN:

1. The compulsory televised death match depicted in Suzanne Collins' popular trilogy

2. Above average people are forced to wear these in Vonnegut's short story *Harrison Bergeron*

3. Insect-like alien race in Orson Scott Card's *Ender's Game*

4. In this Mike Judge film, today's citizens of average intelligence are geniuses in the future

5. Mask worn by the anarchist revolutionary in Alan Moore's *V for Vendetta*

6. Ruling class of men in Margaret Atwood's *The Handmaid's Tale*

9. A misprint results in the death of cobbler Archibald Buttle instead of suspected terrorist Archibald Tuttle in this 1985 film

11. Egg hunters in Ernest Cline's *Ready Player One*

13. Antagonists in H.G. Wells' 1895 novel *The Time Machine*

15. Headwear donned by "the Strangers" in the film *Dark City*

ACROSS:

7. In *They Live*, a drifter's discovery of this object enables him to see an alien race, disguised as humans, that is planting subliminal messages as a form of thought control

8. Dictatorial leader of Oceania in George Orwell's *Nineteen Eighty-Four*

9. Items being burned in Ray Bradbury's *Fahrenheit 451*

10. Psychics in *Minority Report* who stop crime before it happens

12. 1997 film in which Vincent Freeman's dreams of space travel are threatened due to his "in-valid" status

14. Corporation that solves its ocean plankton supply chain issues with the use of human corpses

16. Fritz Lang's 1927 silent film, regarded as a pioneering science-fiction movie

17. Isaac Asimov's chief robopsychologist at U.S. Robots and Mechanical Men, Inc. in *I, Robot*

18. An annual holiday where, for a 12-hour period, crime is legal

19. 1978 Stephen King novel in which a mega-virus wipes out most of humanity

DYSTOPIAN FICTION CROSSWORD: PUZZLE

CRYPTOGRAMS: WE'RE GONNA NEED A DRINK EDITION

Decode the message! Each letter in the phrase has been replaced with a random number. Try to decode the message using the clues that have already been revealed!

A	B	C	D	E	F	G	H	I	J	K	L	M	N	O	P	Q	R	S	T	U	V	W	X	Y	Z
								8											15			24			

W H A T (24 12 20 15) **K I N D** (9 8 10 26) **O F** (19 4)

W I N E (24 8 10 5) **G O E S** (25 19 5 21) **W I T H** (24 8 15 12)

W A T C H I N G (24 20 15 6 12 8 10 25) **T H E** (15 12 5)

D O W N F A L L (26 19 24 10 4 20 7 7) **O F** (19 4)

S O C I E T Y (21 19 6 8 5 15 23)

53

WORRIED? YOU SHOULD BE!

Society headed downhill fast? Of course it is! Make a list of all the ways things will get worse in the years to come. Worry about it now and brag about being right later!

BUNKERING ON A BUDGET

Will humanity destroy the world with our unquenchable thirst for violence? Probably. It's only a matter of time before our governments decide to go nuclear on each other again, so plan accordingly. You have a budget of $2000 to outfit your fallout shelter with essentials. Shop from the menu below and on the next page and spend exactly $2000 on your supplies.

FOOD & DRINK
- Canned peas $20
- Canned tuna $30
- Canned fruit $20
- Mixed veggies $20
- Canned soup $25
- Protein bars $65
- Crackers $15
- Candy $15
- Mixed nuts $30
- Drinking water $100
- Instant coffee $15
- Energy drinks $60
- Whiskey $75
- Vodka $75

TECHNOLOGY & TOOLS
- Walkie talkies $100
- Radio $30
- Broadcasting equipment $200
- Generator and fuel $750
- Camping stove $40
- Radiation kit $50
- Flashlight and flares $30
- Batteries $30
- Tool box $65
- Can opener $10

BUNKERING ON A BUDGET (CONT'D)

CREATURE COMFORTS
- Towels $20
- Sheets & pillows $50
- Sleeping bags $200

ENTERTAINMENT
- Puzzles $20
- Card & board games $50
- Books $75
- DVDs & DVD player $100
- Condoms* $50

PERSONAL CARE
- First aid kit $25
- Shampoo & conditioner $15
- Soap $10
- Antibiotics $30
- Vitamins $10
- Bleach $10
- Trash bags $20
- Toilet paper & paper towels $30
- Toothbrushes, tooth paste, and dental floss $10
- Cyanide capsules** $30

PERSONAL DEFENSE
- Rifle & ammunition $200
- Knives & scissors $50
- Fire extinguisher $50

* Or some other reliable form of birth control in the event that you end up trapped with a fertile member of the opposing gender, happen to be attracted to them, and everyone involved is an enthusiastically consenting adult. We know the temptation to re-populate the planet will be strong; resist it! Too many humans competing for finite resources is what got you into this mess. Besides, a shrieking infant is the last thing you want around if you're trying to escape the notice of the cannibalistic mutant marauders wandering the wasteland outside.

** Look, it's a nuclear apocalypse out there. No one's gonna judge you if you decide after a few years (or days) to bounce a little early. Besides, unless you're sticking around to help clean up, being the last guest at the party is very gauche.

MATH PUZZLE: GILDED GROCERIES

Thanks to a perfect hell storm of inflation and droughts, groceries will only get more expensive in the future. Solve the puzzle below to see what the average monthly grocery bill will be in the future for a family of four!

🍎 + 🍎 + 4 = 🍌

(🍎 + 4) × 🍞 = 7,000

🍞 ÷ 🍌 = 🍒

🍒 ÷ 4 = 🧀

7,000 + 🍒 + 🧀 = ?

HOPELESS HAIKU: BUGGIN' OUT EDITION

Add some beauty to this little corner of the abyss with poetry! On this page, write a haiku about giant mutant insects created by an industrial pesticide mishap.

Tip: Haiku is a Japanese poetic form comprised of three lines. The first line has five syllables, the second line has seven syllables, and the last line has five syllables.

_____

_____

_____

FUTURE NEWS: BIRTHDAY BASH

Fill in the blanks below with the requested word or phrase. Then plug those words into the corresponding blanks on the next page to complete the news article from the future! *(Note: This activity is best done with a friend/captive.)*

Adjective: _____

Place: _____

Adjective: _____

Number: _____

Number: _____

Noun: _____

Famous Villain: _____

Famous Villain: _____

Famous Villain: _____

Animal: _____

Object (plural): _____

Dead Rock Star: _____

Verb: _____

Noun: _____

Adjective: _____

Food: _____

Noun: _____

Adjective: _____

Verb (ending in "ing"): _____

Noun: _____

JEFF BEZOS CELEBRATES 400TH BIRTHDAY WITH A 10 BILLION DOLLAR BASH ON MARS

Amazon founder, _____ supervillain, and former Ambassador to _____ Jeff Bezos threw a _____ party for _____ guests at his _____ trillion dollar compound that encompasses the entire planet of Mars. The former executive and current _____ turned 400 on January 12th.

In attendance were _____, _____, and _____. Bezos spent approximately 10 billion dollars on his party, having _____ entertainers, a 500-foot pit of _____, and a surprise performance by the reanimated corpse of _____.

Bezos and his guests broadcast highlights from the celebration on his newest social media platform _____ _____ as a treat for the remaining denizens of the _____ Earth. Footage of the party revealed an endless buffet of _____, which is Bezos' favorite and only source of sustenance.

Planche Bezos, the 201st wife to Mr. Bezos, posted that evening to Instagag "My dearest Jeff is the _____ of my life. I am so thankful to be enjoying this _____ day with him." Her body was found the following morning _____ in a dumpster.

A representative for the Bezos _____ has offered no comment at this time.

Y'ALL NEED REBUS

Rebus puzzles use words and/or images to convey a message. Below you'll find 10 rebus puzzles that reveal dystopian words and phrases.

Y'ALL NEED REBUS (CONT'D)

6. [ballot] + [lute] =

7. Re + [iron] + ion =

8. [running person] + [switch OFF] =

9. [tie] + [running person] + [heel] =

10. [watermelon] + [collie] =

CLIMATE CRISIS CROSSWORD: CLUES

Climate scientists have been sounding the alarm bell for decades, but has this stopped humanity from destroying the only planet we call home? Of course it hasn't! While our dumb species continues to wreck the Earth, we can kill some time solving this crossword puzzle that reminds us of our impending doom.

DOWN:

1. Petroleum company mishaps which dump sludge into water, causing contamination & danger to wildlife

2. Chopping down trees to make room for ranches, farms, and urban use

3. Waste resulting from nuclear power; known to cause cancer and Godzilla

4. Part of Earth's stratosphere that absorbs ultraviolet radiation from the Sun

6. Not-so-"great" patch in the Pacific estimated to be double the size of Texas

10. More than 99% of all species on Earth have suffered this fate

12. Loss in vegetation associated with increases in dust emissions and dust storms

14. A new life for items like paper, bottles, and cans (if only we'd bother to do it)

16. Gas that absorbs & emits radiant energy within the thermal infrared range, such as carbon dioxide, methane, or nitrous oxide

17. Water containing wastes from residential, commercial, and industrial processes

ACROSS:

5. Urban haze associated with coal combustion, vehicular & industrial emissions, forest & agricultural fires, and photochemical reactions of those emissions

7. Environmental phenomena caused by emissions of sulphur dioxide & nitrogen oxide

8. Popular 20th century fire-resistant building material associated with cancer

9. Energy sources such as sunlight, wind, rain, tides, waves, and geothermal heat

11. Extreme weather and rising sea levels are only going to make it worse

13. Melting them causes rising sea levels, coastal erosion, and storm surges

15. Species likely to become extinct

18. An April observance where humans pretend to care about planting trees

19. Standards limiting the amount of air pollutants that may be released by vehicles

20. Oldest & most common form of waste disposal

21. Hydraulic petroleum & natural gas extraction method associated with earthquakes and air & water pollution

CLIMATE CRISIS CROSSWORD: PUZZLE

WORD SEARCH: MODERN MISERY

Modern technology was supposed to make our lives easier, but of course it's just made everything worse. Find the misery in 21st century life in the puzzle below!

```
F Y K L P T R W V D H S F P D N T A X
U T N T H T G P Q O P A B X A O U L U Q
I W U I O F R V H O M E T A V E R S E A
E I L V M P O I P O G Z G A B N V D F M
J T D S J W U R F A N Y L L B Q H V I A
O T T E Q S P T A S L E M G X R Z H Q Z
I E E C O E T U C O Z P T O Y P E M M O
C R L U K L E A E C O Q S R D W M A Y N
Y B E R E F X L B I O K N I E K K B C O
B F M I V I T R O A M R S T V E D I S H
E V A T I E K E O L I Q T H H S O O P C
R P R Y K S K A K M I H P M H C O M Y C
B A K P I N F L U E N C E R S R M E W A
U S E A H N Q I Y D C U X M I E S T A P
L S T T D M C T F I O V A Q Q E C R R T
L W E C E S N Y S A L B G Y W N R I E C
Y O R H L Z P Y V D I W A L W T O C K H
I R S Q J S U A B K T U S D A I L X C A
N D H L B L Q D M Y O F F D Z M L Q P X
G S K T R O L L S M K J A C D E M B R V
```

Virtual Reality	Cyberbullying	Security Patch	Social Media
Influencers	Telemarketers	Data Breach	Doom Scroll
Screen Time	Phone Tree	Metaverse	Biometric
Algorithm	Captcha	Selfies	Twitter
Trolls	Spam	Passwords	Group Text
Facebook	Spyware	Amazon	Zoom

THERE *IS* A PLANET B!
(AND THE "B" STANDS FOR "BOY, DOES THIS PLACE SUCK COMPARED TO THE LAST ONE")

With our reckless disregard for the environment, humanity has finally made Earth uninhabitable. The good news is we've found a new planet to ruin! The bad news is the new planet is decidedly sub-optimal. Fill in the details below about humanity's mediocre new home planet.

Name
(Name our new planetary abode, preferably something more creative than "Earth II.")

Climate/Seasons
(Always just a little too dry or in a perpetual state of drizzle? What are the weather and seasons like?)

Wildlife
(Who or what else lives on the new planet with us? Giant insects? Fire-breathing birds? Describe the denizens of our new dwelling below.)

Plant Life
(What sort of vegetation grows on our new planet? Flesh-eating flowers? Funky, foul-smelling trees? Describe our fresh batch of flora below.)

Cuisine
(What is there to eat on the new planet? Flaming hot grains? Psychedelic fruit? What will we be munching on as we slowly ruin this place?)

Dangers
(What hazards lurk in our new world? Do we have to watch out for sand tsunamis or were-goat attacks? Jot it down here!)

Additional Features
(What else is totally f**ked about our new home? So-so gravity that causes chronic bad hair days? Cloud formations that emit an eardrum-shattering mating call? Use your imagination and write down your worst case scenarios below!)

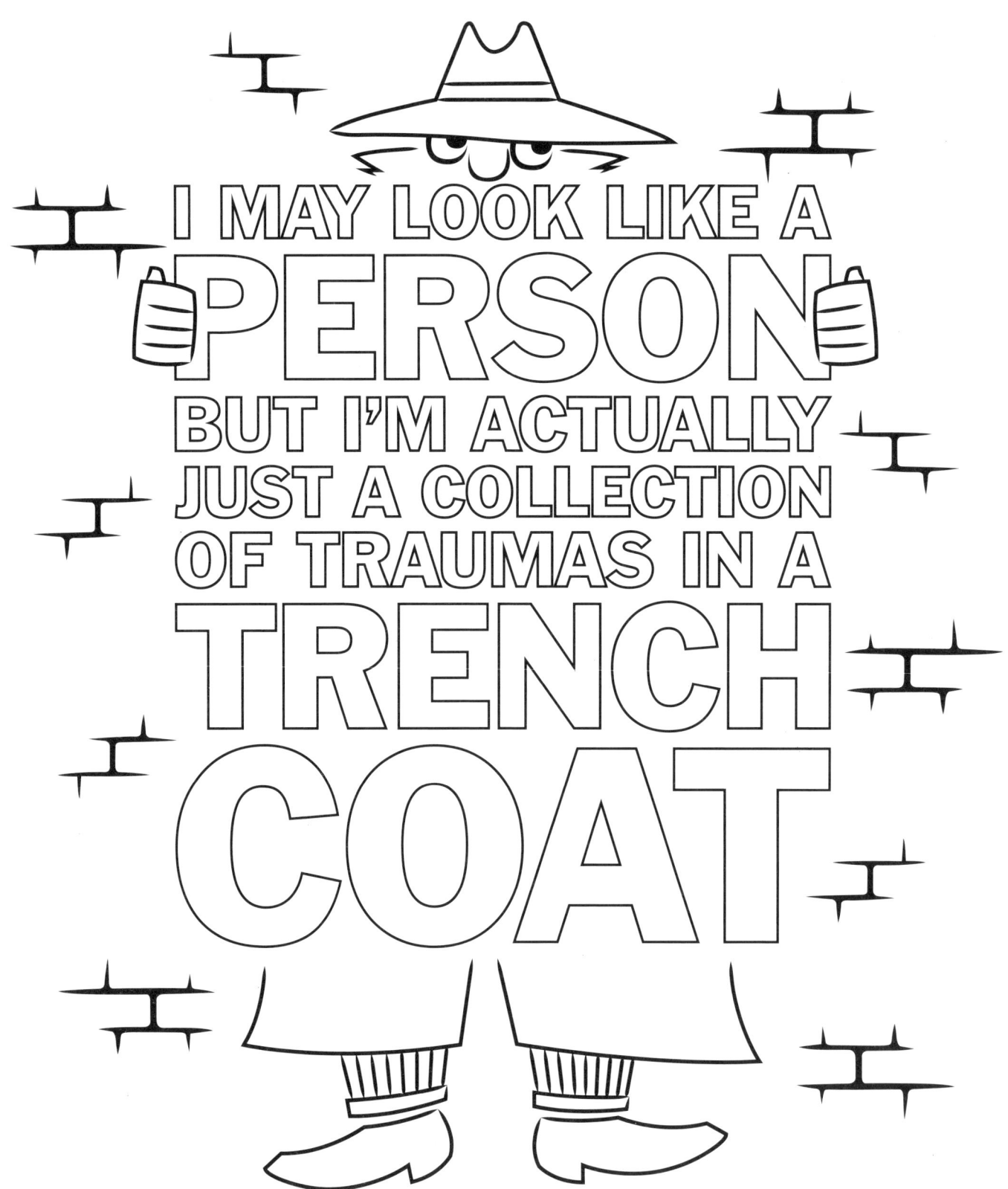

IT'S GO TIME!

Whether your future involves fleeing a despotic government or World War III, it's only a matter of time before you'll need a well-stocked "go-bag." Prepare your go-bag list below so you'll have a duffel at the ready that you can quickly grab as you run for the border or bunker!

TWO TRUTHS AND ONE LIE (PART 2)

In each puzzle below you'll find two true headlines and one that's made up. Identify the fake one!

PUZZLE 1

a.) Influencer sells vials of her blood to a fan for $100,000

b.) Australian Prime Minister asks states to allow children to drive forklifts to ease labor shortage

c.) A.I. start-up contracts with state law enforcement agencies to predict crime and catch perpetrators before it happens

PUZZLE 2

a.) A South Dakota arena to hold a "Dash for Cash" where teachers get on their knees and fight for one dollar bills that they can use for classroom supplies while spectators watch and cheer

b.) Dallas woman fired from accounting firm for not smiling more

c.) Bay Area start-up deploys robots to harass homeless

PUZZLE 3

a.) Chilean sports fans delighted as dead soccer player in coffin scores goal

b.) Injured worker sent repair bill for forklift that malfunctioned

c.) Factory workers threatened with firing if they left to flee oncoming tornado

PUZZLE 4

a.) Texas says it will limit the number of voter registration forms it can give out due to supply chain issues

b.) YouTuber suspected of intentionally crashing plane for views

c.) Alaska town elects a robot to city council

TWO TRUTHS AND ONE LIE (PART 2, CONT'D)

In each puzzle below you'll find two true headlines and one that's made up. Identify the fake one!

PUZZLE 1

a.) Woman billed $700 after sitting in ER waiting room for 7 hours and leaving without treatment

b.) Billionaires clone themselves to generate the "perfect heirs" to their fortunes

c.) Georgia bans giving water to people waiting in line to vote

PUZZLE 2

a.) Creator of dystopian sci-fi TV show says reality is too bleak to make another season of the show

b.) Amazon workers urinated in empty bottles due to inability to take bathroom breaks

c.) U.S. eyes a "labor draft" to increase workforce participation

PUZZLE 3

a.) Start-up to facilitate the sale of human kidneys secures venture capital investment

b.) Arizona plans to use same deadly gas used at Auschwitz to execute prisoners

c.) Company spends $5.5M to advertise a $1M charity donation

PUZZLE 4

a.) 7 year old faces life behind bars after second accidental shooting

b.) LAPD arrests Black man during search for white suspect

c.) Man locked up in mental hospital in Hawaii for two years in case of mistaken identity

LOGIC PUZZLE: CORPORATE GREED

If there's one thing we can count on in our modern waking nightmare, it's that the rich keep getting richer. Determine the value of these mega corps in 100 years! Below you'll see the dossiers on each of these corporate creeps:

Nestlé
- Founded: 1866
- Founder(s): Henri Nestlé
- HQ: Vevey, Vaud, Switzerland

AT&T
- Founded: 1885
- Founder(s): Alexander Graham Bell and Gardiner Greene Hubbard
- HQ: Dallas, Texas, United States

Walmart
- Founded: 1962
- Founder(s): Sam Walton
- HQ: Bentonville, Arkansas, United States

Microsoft
- Founded: 1975
- Founder(s): Bill Gates and Paul Allen
- HQ: Redmond, Washington, United States

Amazon
- Founded: 1994
- Founder(s): Jeff Bezos
- HQ: Seattle, Washington, United States

Google
- Founded: 1998
- Founder(s): Larry Page and Sergey Brin
- HQ: Mountain View, California, United States

ExxonMobil
- Founded: 1999
- Founder(s): John D. Rockefeller (originally incorporated as Standard Oil in 1870)
- HQ: Irving, Texas, United States

JPMorgan Chase
- Founded: 2000
- Founder(s): Aaron Burr, Balthazar Melick, John Pierpont Morgan, John Thompson
- HQ: New York City, New York, United States

LOGIC PUZZLE: CORPORATE GREED

- The least valuable company's name starts with a vowel
- The two most valuable companies have the letter M in their name
- All Texas-based companies are worth less than $10T each
- The most valuable company has a two-syllable name
- US-based companies based in west coast states are all worth over $20T
- All companies founded in the 1990s are worth over $5T
- All companies with Johns as founders are worth over $3.5T and under $10T
- All companies worth over $50T have a only one founder
- The third most valuable company is older than the fourth most valuable company

	Nestlé	AT&T	Walmart	Microsoft	Amazon	Google	ExxonMobil	JPMorgan Chase
$3T								
$4T								
$9T								
$12T								
$30T								
$40T								
$99T								
$100T								

CRYPTOGRAMS: ENDLESS DESPAIR EDITION

Decode the message! Each letter in the phrase has been replaced with a random number. Try to decode the message using the clues that have already been revealed!

A	B	C	D	E	F	G	H	I	J	K	L	M	N	O	P	Q	R	S	T	U	V	W	X	Y	Z
				10			3	18																	

$\underset{1}{\_}\ \underset{3}{H}\ \underset{18}{I}\ \underset{4}{\_}\ \underset{16}{\_}\ \underset{23}{\_}$ $\underset{11}{\_}\ \underset{18}{I}\ \underset{16}{\_}\ \underset{3}{H}\ \underset{1}{\_}$

$\underset{25}{\_}\ \underset{10}{E}\ \underset{10}{E}\ \underset{14}{\_}$ $\underset{3}{H}\ \underset{5}{\_}\ \underset{20}{\_}\ \underset{10}{E}\ \underset{14}{\_}\ \underset{10}{E}\ \underset{23}{\_}\ \underset{23}{\_}$

$\underset{4}{\_}\ \underset{5}{\_}\ \underset{24}{\_}$ $\underset{19}{\_}\ \underset{26}{\_}\ \underset{1}{\_}$ $\underset{15}{\_}\ \underset{5}{\_}\ \underset{4}{\_}\ \text{'}\ \underset{1}{\_}$

$\underset{24}{\_}\ \underset{5}{\_}\ \underset{6}{\_}\ \underset{6}{\_}\ \underset{22}{\_}$ $\underset{1}{\_}\ \underset{3}{H}\ \underset{10}{E}\ \underset{22}{\_}\ \text{'}\ \underset{14}{\_}\ \underset{14}{\_}$

$\underset{25}{\_}\ \underset{10}{E}\ \underset{10}{E}\ \underset{14}{\_}$ $\underset{3}{H}\ \underset{5}{\_}\ \underset{20}{\_}\ \underset{10}{E}\ \underset{14}{\_}\ \underset{10}{E}\ \underset{23}{\_}\ \underset{23}{\_}$

$\underset{14}{\_}\ \underset{2}{\_}\ \underset{1}{\_}\ \underset{10}{E}\ \underset{6}{\_}$ $\underset{1}{\_}\ \underset{5}{\_}\ \underset{5}{\_}$

PARTY LIKE IT'S 2099!

Haha, no way is our species making it to 2099. In any event, the apocalypse is nigh, and you get to DJ at the end of the world! Which songs belong on the soundtrack? Compile an epic doomsday playlist below!

Examples:
'It's the End of the World As We Know It (And I Feel Fine)' - R.E.M.
'Ghost Town' - The Specials
'Don't Fear The Reaper' - Blue Öyster Cult
'Black Hole Sun' - Soundgarden

1. _____
2. _____
3. _____
4. _____
5. _____
6. _____
7. _____
8. _____
9. _____
10. _____
11. _____
12. _____
13. _____
14. _____
15. _____
16. _____
17. _____
18. _____
19. _____
20. _____
21. _____
22. _____
23. _____
24. _____
25. _____
26. _____
27. _____
28. _____
29. _____
30. _____

HIDDEN HORRORS!

Each sentence below has a hidden dystopian word within it. Find each of them!

Example*: I **hope less** people are born this year, it will be less people to suffer through existence in the future.* **(Hopeless. The answer is hopeless. Like humanity's future!)**

1. Panic episodes paired with hopelessness is what modern existence is all about.

2. A firenado, a fire/tornado hybrid, is a stern warning to us all about the future of our climate.

3. If you'd read the news recently, you'd be worried about the future, too.

4. Today's trouble, akin to something from a horror movie, is all too real unfortunately.

HIDDEN HORRORS! (CONT'D)

5. Here's your clue: there's a reason separation of church and state is a good idea.

6. The forecast every day gets more alarming, as climate change leads to more floods and extreme weather.

7. At this age, no ciders or beers for me; instead of taking the edge off it will just give me a hangover.

8. If you don't agree, don't speak up; the subjugators aren't listening, anyway.

SIX WORD STORIES

Flex your creative muscles with the easiest of storytelling — distill these doom and gloom story ideas into just six words.

1. Write a six word short story about how the world finally ends.
Example: The great garbage heap buries humanity.

2. Write a six word short story about the rise of a new dictator.
Example: We voted, but it didn't matter.

SIX WORD STORIES (CONT'D)

Flex your creative muscles with the easiest of storytelling — distill these doom and gloom story ideas into just six words.

1. Write a six word short story about a billionaire's visit to space.
Example: Good luck, Mars. Please keep Elon.

2. Write a six word short story about a new highly contagious virus.
Example: First came hives, then came chaos.

WORD JUMBLE: MODERN TECHNOLOGY

Unscramble the words in the modern technology themed puzzle below:

1. aiuvlrt aelyrti

2. ewtrtti

3. modo locrls

4. wsdrpoas

5. igmasnrta

6. oilsac iaedm

7. gporu xett

8. laiem

9. rcbye tankilsg

10. ckoabfeo

11. rtcdei aemgses

12. atnirkcg

13. sslefei

14. lneeniucfr

15. kcbol nahic

16. yirapvc yciopl

MATH PUZZLE: END OF THE WORLD

Want to feel like Nostradamus? Solve the puzzle below to reveal the year that the world will end.

$$(\text{8ball} - 80) \div \text{eye} = \text{fire}$$

$$\text{fire} \times 1{,}000 = \text{meteor}$$

$$1{,}000 \div \text{eye} = \text{8ball}$$

$$\text{8ball} - (\text{fire} \times \text{eye}) = 80$$

$$\text{meteor} + \text{8ball} + 80 = \text{?}$$

HOPELESS HAIKU: CATACLYSMIC COMET EDITION

Add some beauty to this little corner of the abyss with poetry! On this page, write a haiku about the comet that ends it all.

Tip: Haiku is a Japanese poetic form comprised of three lines. The first line has five syllables, the second line has seven syllables, and the last line has five syllables.

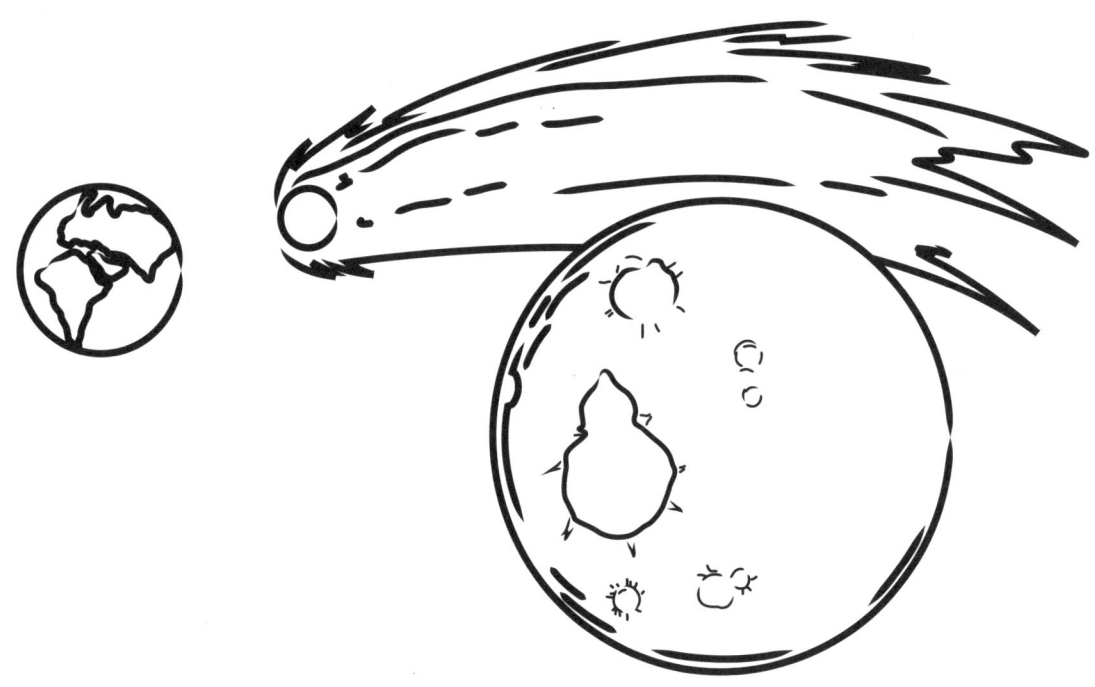

WORD SEARCH: OPPRESSION SESSION

Find the examples of social and/or political oppression in the puzzle below!

```
C L S M C G D Y P R O P A G A N D A J D
V K S I E W P E M O Y E O W D Y Y H B Q
A O J R M T V E H A L C T P H A H J S S
U C T P C P H O R C R I W T Q I T D F I
T K O E F H E N B S L T C C G Z A M A N
H S H L R N O R I I E L I E A Q N N S E
O Y O C O S P M I C L C K A S P U D C Q
R Z L G K N U L O A C O U P L T I D I U
I O O E U A I P U P L L L T K L A O S A
T R C N B Z S A P T H I E I I S A T M L
A Z A O M L Z P L R O O S A G O V W E I
R P U C Q Q U A N I E C B M N A N Y W T
I O S I I X J R M B S S R I J S R E A Y
A V T D Y S K T J Z G M S A A U I C R Y
N E H E V R M H Z E Y N T I C Q Y N H I
I R O N D G O E W S B W U I O Y H X G Y
S T A P M P X I L T K X J S W N P S U B
M Y A C I B W D D I C T A T O R S H I P
G C E N S O R S H I P H E G E M O N Y V
K B A F M L X V G L T H E O C R A C Y N
```

Voter Suppression	Authoritarianism	Persecution	Police State
Imperialism	Dictatorship	Ethnic Cleansing	Censorship
Colonialism	Homophobia	Plutocracy	Propaganda
Martial Law	Theocracy	Apartheid	Genocide
Racism	Oligarchy	Hegemony	Fascism
Inequality	Holocaust	Poverty	War

FUTURE NEWS: CONGRESSIONAL CREEPS

Fill in the blanks below with the requested word or phrase. Then plug those words into the corresponding blanks on the next page to complete the news article from the future! *(Note: This activity is best done with a friend/captive.)*

Noun: _____

Adjective: _____

Animal: _____

Noun: _____

State: _____

Verb (ending in "ing"): _____

Verb (ending in "ing"): _____

Verb (ending in "ing"): _____

Female Celebrity: _____

Adjective: _____

Adjective: _____

Adjective: _____

Celebrity: _____

Noun: _____

Adjective: _____

Number (1-100): _____

Verb: _____

Place: _____

Form of Punishment: _____

Technology: _____

Number (1-100): _____

CONGRESS CALLS FOR CITIZENS TO BE MONITORED BY CAMERAS AT HOME

The Congressional _____ Caucus has proposed a bill that would mandate the installation of security cameras in the homes of private citizens by the year 2085. Calling the measure "necessary and _____," Congressman _____ _____ of _____ told reporters Wednesday that the measure would ensure greater security for the nation.

"Right now, you've got people in their homes doing who knows what! They could be _____, _____, or _____! We just don't know! But with these new cameras we'll be able to keep an eye on it," said Congresswoman _____.

Opponents of the legislation have argued that the measure is _____ and _____. Before his _____ disappearance, civil rights activist _____ called the proposal a "gross overreach" and stated it would likely only worsen the _____ crisis, a problem many _____ voters are particularly concerned with.

Some lawmakers have questioned the costs involved with the measure, suggesting implementation could cost tax payers at least _____ billion dollars. Congressmen _____ _____ told reporters that taxpayer funds would be better suited funding efforts like _____ or _____.

The bill is set to go to the floor for debate as early as next month, with insiders suggesting it has at least a _____% chance of passing during this legislative session.

CRUEL WORLD CROSSWORD: CLUES

With rising wealth inequality, environmental destruction, and an expected increase in global pandemics and political unrest, there are plenty of reasons to despair. Distract yourself from the hellscape with this puzzle about the futility of everything!

DOWN:

1. Slang for "lowest point"

2. Nasty comments about how you look

5. Not-so-sweet dreams

6. 1987 Stephen King novel

7. Famously depressed author of *The Bell Jar*

8. The glass is half empty

11. Physically and emotionally tired

13. Imagining worst case scenarios

18. Overthinking

19. In 2017 the FBI released new data showing a 17% increase in this type of crime between 2016 and 2017

20. Psychiatrist, informally

24. The Sackler family got rich and America got a crisis

25. Sometimes I worry there's something I'm forgetting to worry about

ACROSS:

3. Post _____ Stress Disorder

4. No-contact with toxic relatives

9. That mean voice in your head

10. Gloom's companion

11. Dissatisfaction, but make it French

12. Nothing is ever good enough

14. Actually, it *is* the end of the world

15. Syndrome, opposite of Dunning-Krueger

16. In 2021 Tetsushi Sakamoto was appointed Japan's first minister of it

17. Death of oyster boy

19. Four _____ of the Apocalypse

21. The Smiths' 1987 single that put DJs on edge

22. Sisyphus' quest

23. It'll keep you safe from a pandemic, but depression, not so much

CRUEL WORLD CROSSWORD: PUZZLE

CRYPTOGRAMS: NO TRUTH IN ADVERTISING EDITION

Decode the message! Each letter in the phrase has been replaced with a random number. Try to decode the message using the clues that have already been revealed!

A	B	C	D	E	F	G	H	I	J	K	L	M	N	O	P	Q	R	S	T	U	V	W	X	Y	Z
				20				24																	

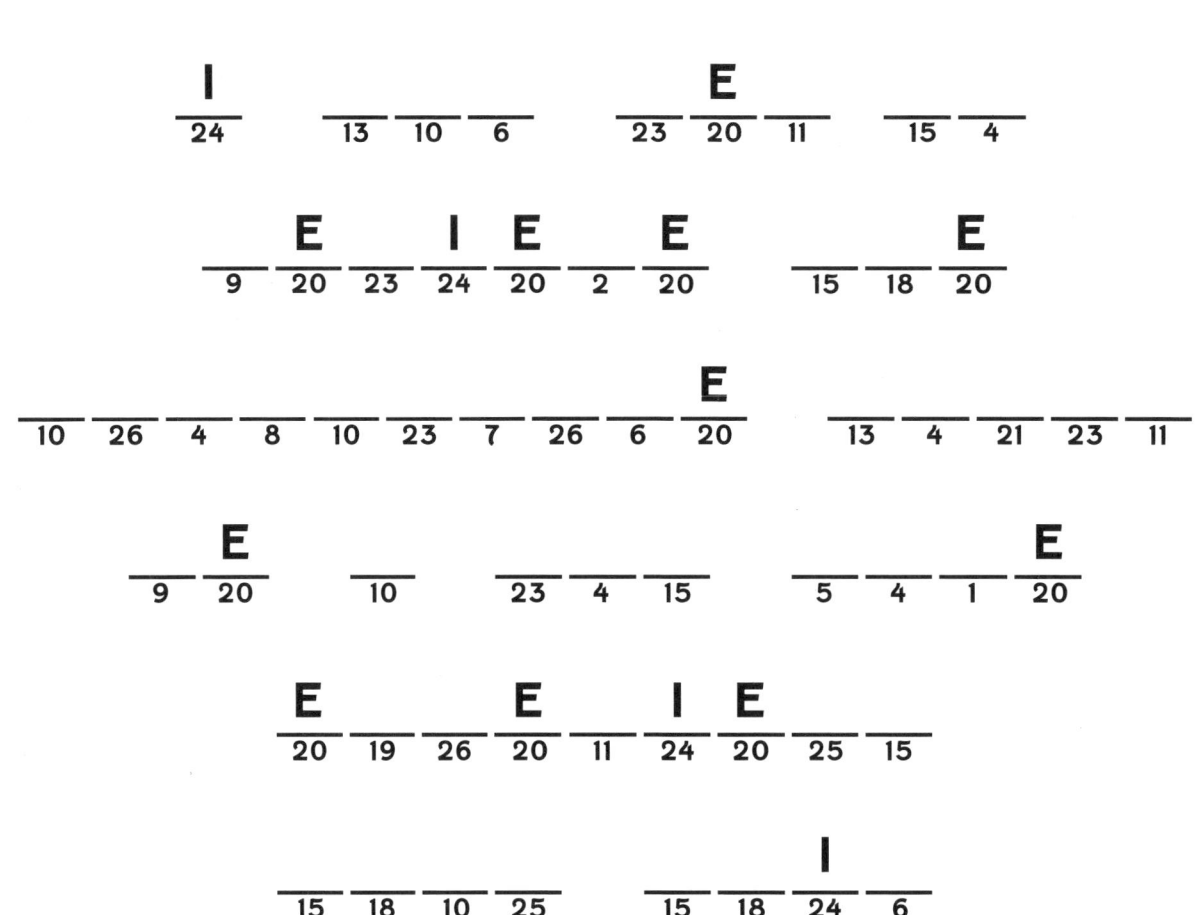

ANSWER KEY

Down in the dumps because you're still stumped? Fair enough; this has been a harrowing ordeal for all of us (and by "this" we mean existence). The answers you seek can be found below and on the following pages:

Word Search:
Sorrowful Saga
(Page 1)

```
H Q D E P R E S S I O N V U B
E N N U I I S O L A T I O N L
W K S E L F L O A T H I N G E
I A S U F F E R I N G W Q N A
L D Y S F U N C T I O N I B K
L D K X V S E R O T O N I N C
T Y T F Z D O P A M I N E B R
O S T R A U M A N X I E T Y I
L T D I S T R E S S D O O M S
I O R E J E C T I O N D E E I
V P J P A N I C C R Y I N G S
E I P E S S I M I S M N F M O
M A W G H H E L L S C A P E F
D I S A P P O I N T M E N T Q
M I S E R Y Z H O P E L E S S
```

Math Puzzle:
Gravity
(Page 3)

$10 \times 10 = 100$
$40 \div 10 = 4$
$4 \div 2 = 2$
$100 - (40 \times 2) = 20$
$20 + 2 = 22$
$100 + 22 = 122$

Crossword:
Toxic Tech
(Pages 7-8)

Down

1. scammers
2. urban
3. YouTubers
5. metaverse
6. data breach
8. swiping
11. clickbait
12. telemarketers
14. likes
15. cookies
16. slacktivism
19. disinformation
22. billionaires
25. catfishing

Across

4. multitasking
7. trolls
9. hackers
10. comments
11. crypto
13. influencers
17. phone tree
18. revenge
20. corporations
21. inbox
23. screentime
24. Facebook
26. spam

Spot The Difference #1
(Page 9)

Spot The Difference #2
(Page 10)

ANSWER KEY

Word Jumble: Dystopian Authors (Page 12)

1. George Orwell
2. Margaret Atwood
3. Ray Bradbury
4. H.G. Wells
5. Anthony Burgess
6. Philip K. Dick
7. Ernest Cline
8. Suzanne Collins
9. Aldous Huxley
10. Sinclair Lewis
11. Ursula K. Le Guin
12. John Wyndham
13. Franz Kafka
14. David Foster Wallace
15. Kurt Vonnegut
16. William Golding

Hell World Homographs (Pages 13-14)

1. minute
2. content
3. desert
4. discount
5. refuse
6. subject
7. club
8. book
9. bank
10. ring

Maze: Phone Tree Trap (Page 15)

Cryptograms: De-Motivational Quote Edition (Page 17)

Despair like no one is watching.

Math Puzzle: Trillionaires (Page 22)

5 + 5 = 10
5 x 10 = 50
50 x 10 = 500
500 x 10 = 5000
5000 + 500 + 10 = 5510

Who Said It? (Page 20)

1. Philip K. Dick
2. Friedrich Nietzsche
3. Margaret Atwood
4. H.G. Wells
5. George Orwell
6. T.S. Eliot
7. Henry David Thoreau
8. L.M. Montgomery
9. Charles Dickens
10. Kurt Vonnegut
11. Aldous Huxley

Cryptograms: Corner Office In Hell Edition (Page 21)

Another meeting that could have been an ineffectual scream into the void.

Crossword: Hellscape History (Pages 23-24)

Down	Across
1. Genghis Khan	7. Anthony (Susan B.)
2. Black Death	8. Galileo
3. Henry VIII	9. children
4. gladiators	11. Lavender Scare
5. Bloodletting	13. internment
6. Pinochet	14. Jackson (Andrew)
10. Mao	15. guillotine
12. MK Ultra	16. napalm
17. shellshock	17. slavery
18. pillory	19. Tiananmen
20. Nero	21. serfs
	22. Joan of Arc

ANSWER KEY

**Logic Puzzle:
Horrible History Reborn
(Pages 25-26)**

First: Elizabeth Báthory

Second: Mao Zedong

Third: Attila the Hun

Fourth: Vladimir Lenin

Fifth: Genghis Khan

Sixth: Joseph Stalin

Seventh: Vlad the Impaler

**Misspelling Misery
(Page 27)**

1. authoretarian (*authoritarian*)
2. catastraphe (*catastrophe*)
3. dispair (*despair*)
4. feifdom (*fiefdom*)
5. hysetria (*hysteria*)
6. inquisiition (*inquisition*)
7. melancholly (**melancholy**)
8. nuclaer waste (*nuclear waste*)
9. polllution (*pollution*)
10. sufferring (*suffering*)
11. truama (*trauma*)
12. ventrue capitalist (*venture capitalist*)

**Two Truths & One Lie,
Part 1
(Page 28)**

Puzzle 1: b.

Puzzle 2: c.

Puzzle 3: c.

Puzzle 4: b.

**Word Search:
Misogyny
(Page 31)**

```
E Q C I S M K A H M B J Z A A T R C X Z
C D W O T W U N S H Y S T E R I A L X N
U M F P N M B V Y S K N I X V C Y Y H W
S X Y T O Y R H N D A M A N S P L A I N
C R P G R R K D K S L U T S H A M I N G
H O D R O O F I E S W L L V H E G O E R
X A B O R W Z S J I H I M T J Y X Z M M
C V R J U W M M J H H V A B C B Z I F D
M A X A E G D I S C R I M I N A T I O N
H N L G S C H L T D C J B P E U N M A Y
L O C M H S T E M O M M Y T R A C K I M
A S U V D K M I E R E V E N G E P O R N
D M O S Z O F E F Z Q S I R U N R R I S
Y I U W E Y W G N I P A T R I A R C H Y
L S P A S W W N E T C N J U Q P U Z V F
I O S C E X O A I W K A M A L E G A Z E
K C K E X V I R G I N I T Y T E S T E N
E Y I G I M R D K L A K A I N H E K Y O
D N R A S T E A L T H I N G O B D F C Y
Y Y T P M C A T C A L L I N G N I O P D
```

**Word Jumble:
Authoritarian Society
(Page 33)**

1. injustice
2. censorship
3. dictator
4. intimidation
5. fascism
6. propaganda
7. internment
8. martial law
9. oppression
10. persecution
11. totalitarian
12. tyranny
13. surveillance
14. prohibition
15. cruelty
16. intolerance

**Cryptograms:
Already Tired Tomorrow Edition
(Page 34)**

Everything being the absolute worst at all times is exhausting.

ANSWER KEY

Scrambled Rhymes
(Pages 39-40)

1. later dictator
2. glum chum
3. bored horde
4. bleak streak
5. cruel school
6. twitter critter
7. chill pill
8. tomorrow sorrow
9. rude nude
10. trash ash

Word Search: Corporate Dystopia
(Page 41)

Find The Missing Letters
(Pages 45-46)

1. ie
2. ea
3. ll
4. st
5. is
6. or
7. cr
8. fe
9. cy
10. la

Maze: Shelter Search
(Page 48)

Crossword: Dystopian Fiction
(Pages 51-52)

Down
1. Hunger Games
2. handicaps
3. Formics
4. Idiocracy
5. Guy Fawkes
6. Commanders
9. Brazil
11. Gunters
13. Morlocks
15. fedoras

Across
7. Sunglasses
8. Big Brother
9. Books
10. Precogs
14. Soylent
16. Metropolis
17. Calvin
18. The Purge
19. The Stand

Cryptograms: We're Gonna Need A Drink Edition
(Page 53)

What kind of wine goes with watching the downfall of society?

Math Puzzle: Gilded Groceries
(Page 57)

$3 + 3 + 4 = 10$
$(3 + 4) \times 1000 = 7000$
$1000 \div 10 = 100$
$100 \div 4 = 25$
$7000 + 100 + 25 = 7125$

Y'All Need Rebus
(Pages 61-62)

1. Alpaca + Lips = Apocalypse
2. Cat + Ass + Trophy = Catastrophe
3. Hedge + Money = Hegemony
4. Home + Less = Homeless
5. Night + Mare = Nightmare
6. Poll + Lute = Pollute
7. Re + Press + ion = Repression
8. Run + Off = Runoff
9. Tie + Run + Knee = Tyranny
10. Melon + Collie = Melancholy

ANSWER KEY

Crossword: Climate Crisis (Pages 63-64)

Down
1. oil spills
2. deforestation
3. radioactive
4. ozone
6. garbage
10. extinction
12. desertification
14. recycling
16. greenhouse
17. wastewater

Across
5. smog
7. acid rain
8. asbestos
9. renewable
11. flooding
13. ice caps
15. endangered
18. Arbor Day
19. emissions
20. landfill
21. fracking

Word Search: Modern Misery (Page 65)

```
F Y K L P T R W V V D H S F P D N T A X
U T N T H T C R Q O P A B X A O U L U Q
I W U I O F R V H O M E T A V E R S E A
E I L V M P O I P O G Z C A B N V D F M
J T D S J W U R F A N Y L L B Q H V I A
O T T E Q S P T A S L E M C X R Z H Q Z
I E E C O E T U C O Z P T O Y P E M M O
C R L U K L E A E C O Q S R D W M A Y N
Y B E R E F X L B I O K N I E K K B C O
B F M I V I T R O A M R S T V E D I S H
E V A T I E K E O L I Q T H H S O O P C
R P R Y K S K A K M I H P M H C O M Y C
B A K P I N F L U E N C E R S R M E W A
U S E A H N Q I Y D C U X M I E S T A P
L S T T D M C T F I O V A Q Q E C R R T
L W E C E S N Y S A L B C G Y W N R I E C
Y O R H L Z P Y V D I W A L W T O C K H
I R S Q J S U A B K T U S D A I L X C A
N D H L B L Q D M Y O F F D Z M L Q P X
C S K T R O L L S M K J A C D E M B R V
```

Two Truths & One Lie, Part 2 (Page 69)

Puzzle 1: a.

Puzzle 2: b.

Puzzle 3: b.

Puzzle 4: c.

Two Truths & One Lie, Part 3 (Page 70)

Puzzle 1: b.

Puzzle 2: c.

Puzzle 3: a.

Puzzle 4: a.

Logic Puzzle: Corporate Greed (Pages 71-72)

$3T: AT&T
$4T: JPMorgan Chase
$9T: ExxonMobil
$12T: Nestlé
$30T: Google
$40T: Microsoft
$99T: Amazon
$400T: Walmart

Cryptograms: Endless Despair Edition (Page 73)

Things might feel hopeless now, but don't worry, they'll feel hopeless later, too.

Hidden Horrors (Pages 75-76)

1. Panic episo**des pair**ed with hopelessness is what modern existence is all about.
(despair)

2. A firenado, a fire/tornado hybri**d, is a ster**n warning to us all about the future of our climate.
(disaster)

3. If you**'d read** the news recently, you'd be worried about the future, too.
(dread)

4. Today's trou**ble, ak**in to something from a horror movie, is all too real unfortunately.
(bleak)

5. **Here's y**our clue: there's a reason separation of church and state is a good idea.
(heresy)

6. The fore**cast e**very day gets more alarming, as climate change leads to more floods and extreme weather.
(caste)

7. At this a**ge, no cide**rs or beers for me; instead of taking the edge off it will just give me a hangover.
(genocide)

8. If you don't a**gree, d**on't speak up; the subjugators aren't listening, anyway.
(greed)

ANSWER KEY

Word Jumble:
Modern Technology
(Page 79)

1. virtual reality
2. Twitter
3. doom scroll
4. password
5. Instagram
6. social media
7. group text
8. email
9. cyber stalking
10. Facebook
11. direct message
12. tracking
13. selfies
14. influencers
15. block chain
16. privacy policy

Math Puzzle:
End of the World
(Page 80)

$(100 - 80) \div 10 = 2$
$2 \times 1000 = 2000$
$1000 \div 10 = 100$
$100 - (2 \times 10) = 80$
$2000 + 100 + 80 = 2180$

Word Search:
Oppression Session
(Page 82)

```
C L S M C G D Y P R O P A G A N D A J D
V K S I E W P E M O Y E O W D Y Y H B Q
A O J R M T V E H A L C T P H A H J S S
U C T P C P H O R C R I W T Q I T D F I
T K O E F H E N B S L T C C G Z A M A N
H S H L R N O R I E L I E A Q N N S E
O Y O C O S P M I C L C K A S P U D C Q
R Z L C K N U L O A C O U P L T I D I U
I O O E U A I P U R L L T K L A O S A
T R C N B Z S A P T H I E I S A T M L
A Z A O M L Z P L R O O S A G O V W E I
R P U C Q Q U A N I E C B M N A N Y W T
I O S I X J R M B S S R I J S R E A Y
A V T D Y S K T J Z C M S A A U I C R Y
N E H E V R M H Z E Y N T I C Q Y N H I
I R O N D C O E W S B W U I O Y H X C Y
S T A P M P X I L T K X J S W N P S U B
M Y A C I B W D D I C T A T O R S H I P
C E N S O R S H I P H E G E M O N Y E
K B A F M L X V C L T H E O C R A C Y N
```

Crossword:
Cruel World
(Pages 85-86)

Down

1. rock bottom
2. body shaming
5. nightmares
6. misery
7. Plath
8. pessimism
11. exhausted
13. catastrophizing
18. ruminating
19. hate
20. shrink
24. opioid
25. anxiety

Across

3. traumatic
4. estrangement
9. inner critic
10. doom
11. ennui
12. perfectionism
14. apocalypse
15. impostor
16. loneliness
17. melancholy
19. horsemen
21. panic
22. futile
23. isolation

Cryptograms:
No Truth In Advertising Edition
(Page 87)

I was led to believe the apocalypse would be a lot more expedient than this.